C G

THE CLASSICS OF GOLF

Edition of

REMINISCENCES OF GOLF ON ST. ANDREWS LINKS

by

James Balfour

(First published in 1887 by David Douglas)

Foreword by Herbert Warren Wind

Afterword by Jack Nicklaus

ISBN: 0-940889-14-5

Foreword

Far more clearly than any other book written about St. Andrews, James Balfour's "Reminiscences of Golf on St. Andrews Links" quietly explains the deep hold that the Old Course, the Royal and Ancient Golf Club, and the town of St. Andrews come to have on those who play the course steadily over the years. Balfour does not achieve this by any fancy writing. He simply tells you about St. Andrews in seven chapters entitled Links, Balls and Clubs, Medals, Players, Professionals and Caddies, Incidents in Golf, and Merits of the Game. Balfour's attachment to the course, to his golfing friends, and to golf establishes itself profoundly. His book was published in 1887 by the Edinburgh firm of David Douglas, which later that year brought out another notable book on the game, Sir Walter Simpson's "The Art of Golf".

In the early 1840s, when Balfour got to know St. Andrews, not too many people played the course. The only ones who did, as Balfour remarks, were "a few resident gentlemen" and "some occasional strangers" from three other early Scottish courses, Leith, Perth, and Musselburgh. The early golf club was called the Society of St. Andrews Golfers. It did not become the Royal and Ancient Golf Club of St. Andrews until 1834, after Major J. Murray Belshes, an energetic member, had swung into action. He wrote to Sir Herbert Taylor, King William IV's private secretary, suggesting that St. Andrews be made a royal club because of its singular status in the game: in addition to being the second oldest golf club—the Honourable Company of Edinburgh Golfers, founded in 1744, was ten years older—St. Andrews, in the last quarter of the eighteenth century, had come to be regarded by all the other Scottish golf clubs as the leader in the game, and, in the nineteenth century, it had consolidated that position. William IV at length permitted the club to call itself the Royal and Ancient Golf Club of St. Andrews. Major Belshes was then able to persuade the king to become the patron of the club. Midway through the nineteenth century, the imposing sandstone clubhouse was built—a fitting home for the Royal and Ancient, the club responsible for legislating the rules of golf. (In 1854, the year of its centenary anniversary, the club issued a new codification of twenty-two rules that received enthusiastic acceptance.) Today, when golf has swept around the world, the R. & A. remains the game's governing body for all countries except the United States, which, since 1894, has had its own governing body, the United States Golf Association.

All this takes us a good distance from James Balfour and his times. When he set down his reminiscences of St. Andrews in 1887, he had played the Old Course for some forty-five years. In his small world, a great deal had taken place. His book's first chapter, Links, is not hard to read for those who know the present course well enough to have a distinct picture in their mind of each hole, but I have an idea that the opening chapter will be difficult going for people who are not familiar with its layout. St. Andrews is like no other course. When Balfour became a member of the club in 1842, the course consisted of nine narrow holes laid out, as he describes it, "in the shape of a shepherd's crook". At their broadest, the fairways were only forty-five yards wide. When the players had putted out on the ninth green, they turned around and played their way in over the same narrow fairways to the same small greens, and, indeed, putted out into the single cup cut in each green. When they played the tenth, for example, they drove from a small tee off to the side of the ninth green, and played down the ninth fairway to the eighth green, which also served as the tenth green. After they had holed out on the tenth green, they then played the short eleventh. Its brief fairway crossed the seventh fairway, and its green was the well-bunkered seventh green. And so on, down the same fairways and to the same greens that they had used going out but which played altogether differently on the second nine. For example, bunkers which a golfer could safely ignore on the first nine had to be avoided at all cost coming in.

The routing of the holes that James Balfour began to play regularly in 1842 and the present routing of the holes at St. Andrews are, with few exceptions, essentially the same. The first seven holes march north from the town in single file over what for the most part is gently rolling linksland. The next four holes comprise "the loop". The eighth, a par 3, and the ninth, a short par 4 over flat terrain, run from north to south. The tenth, another short par 4, runs from south to north, and the famous eleventh, the second of the course's two par 3s, veers to the northwest. Then the last seven holes march single file back toward the town. At the time Balfour set down his reminiscences, the course had changed quite a bit from the one he had first known. It had been lengthened a bit from the surprisingly long 6,460-yard course he had gotten to know well from 1842 on. (Today, from the championship tees, the course plays to 6,900 yards or thereabouts.) Perhaps the chief change in the routing of the holes, as Balfour brings out, involved the first and second holes. The first green, which had been situated short of the Swilcan Burn and far to the west, close by the seventeenth green, was moved almost a hundred yards to the east and placed just beyond *the burn. (If a member peers through the middle three panels of the bay window of the Big Room in the R. & A. clubhouse, the first tee is almost directly ahead, and so in the distance is the first green some three hundred and seventy yards away, over the burn. It is one of the finest starting holes in golf.) After the new first green was installed, the tee for the second hole was moved to a position just to the right of the first green. This made the second hole appreciably shorter and easier than the old second, but it still requires a nicely played approach shot.*

In both the 1840s and the 1880s, the Old Course demanded exceptional accuracy. It does so today. The player must stay on the fairway. The heavy rough of thick bent, heather, and whins—the regional name for the spiky gorse bush—is not easy to deal with. It is no simple matter to keep the ball on the fairway at St. Andrews because of the strong winds that rush over the treeless course. The course plays at its best when the wind is not behind the golfers—that is, blowing out of the north—on the last seven holes. Then that series of holes comprises one of the very best stretches of golf in all the world. The celebrated hazards on each of them come into play, in varying ways, when an east wind is coming off St. Andrews Bay, or a south wind is blowing dead against the golfers, or a wind out of the west is whistling across the fairways. The golfer then must tack his way skillfully from tee to green, steering clear of such punishing bunkers as Coffin and Lion's Mouth on the thirteenth, the Beardies and Hell on the fourteenth, Sutherland on the fifteenth, the Principal's Nose on the sixteenth, and the Road on the seventeenth. The wind at St. Andrews can shift radically during the course of a round. For example, on the morning that Bobby Jones played his third round on the Old Course in the 1921 British Open, the wind was in his face going out, and then it suddenly shifted a hundred and eighty degrees and blew dead against him coming in.

I have gone into this detail about the routing of St. Andrews in the hope that it may help to clarify

Balfour's detailed description of the course he played as a young man. As he brings out, the course then called for superb control of the ball, the old feather ball—a leather-covered ball stuffed with feathers. The feathery could not be hit anywhere near as far as the ball that began to replace it in 1848, the gutta-percha ball. The gutty was an easier ball for the average golfer to play, but it took skill to maneuver it. Balfour, an able golfer who learned to play the difficult touch shots that the bumpy, tight little course required, wanted to make clear to the reader that the earlier versions of St. Andrews possessed great charm and called for considerable ability with both the feathery and the gutty. The way he felt is the way we all feel about the passions of our youth—the games we played, the songs we sang, the movies we watched, and so on. We resist change, naturally. When it comes, we try to adjust to it, but in a corner of our hearts we feel that things were better in the old days. Let me give you an excellent example of this. Harry Vardon, who won three of his six British Open titles in the 1890s before the rubber-core golf ball replaced the gutta-percha ball, thought that golf was a better game with the gutty. Did anyone else who was close to the game share this opinion? Well, Bernard Darwin also felt that way, and he was a good enough player to reach the semi-finals of the British Amateur, and he watched the play of some remarkable golfers, from Hilton to Hogan, during the forty-five years he served as the golf correspondent of the Times *of London.*

The version of the Old Course that Balfour played when he joined the R. & A. was shortly to change almost beyond recognition. Golf historians tell us that in the 1840s and the years that followed, the width of the fairways was doubled to ninety yards and sometimes to a hundred yards. This enabled each hole to have a fairway of its own. On the first seven holes going out, the golfers used the east side of the fairways. After completing the loop, on the last seven holes they used the west side of the fairways coming in. On some holes, stretches of rough separated the fairway on the east from the fairway on the west. During this period, the greens were also extended, and they became almost as wide as the joint fairways. They became the renowned double greens of St. Andrews. The largest of them, which is shared by the fifth and thirteenth holes, is over an acre in size. The double greens made it possible for each hole to have its own pin position. All in all, there are seven of these sweeping, undulating double greens on the Old Course. Four holes have a green of their own: the first, the ninth, the seventeenth, and the eighteenth. On the second hole through the seventh hole, the golfer played to the pin set on the right side of the green. After completing the loop—he played for the pin on the left on the eighth, tenth, and eleventh—he played for the pin on the right on the ensuing holes as he headed back toward the gray towers of the old town.

Down through the years, changes continued to be made on the Old Course. Some new back tees were added. Some bunkers disappeared. However, one would gather from golf historians, in around 1860 the course had taken on the general aspect that we know today. By that date, the gutta-percha ball had established itself, and for a long time it had no rival. (When you look gutta-percha *up in the dictionary, you learn that it is the solidified form of the latex of certain Malaysian trees of the sapodilla family.) Since the gutty had decidedly different properties from the feathery, it brought about the introduction of golf clubs of a decidedly different design and construction. Balfour begins to get rolling when, in the intimate tone of a diarist, he describes the arrival of such new implements as the Baffing Spoon, the Iron Niblick, the Wooden Niblick, and the Brassy.*

Beginning with the chapter on Balls and Clubs, you are with Balfour at St. Andrews all the way. He tells the reader about the later threat to the gutta-percha ball posed by the Eclipse, a ball made of gutta-percha and of vulcanized India rubber and cork. When he moves on to discuss the fine players of the game, both professional and amateur, he is fully in stride. He gives the reader an excellent appraisal of Andrew Robertson, the first great golfer produced by the links of St. Andrews. He chats about his good friend Old Tom Morris, and adds in a footnote at the end of the second chapter that he had read the first two chapters of this book to Tom Morris, "and he indorses every word of them." Old Tom, who won the Open in 1861, 1862, 1864, and 1868, was the custodian of the Old Course at this time, and he would remain so until his death in 1908. Balfour talks about the caddies at St. Andrews. Many of them were colorful fellows, but in his opinion "perhaps the greatest character among them was 'Lang Willie'. He was very tall, about six feet two, with bent knees and a slouching gait, a tall, swallow-tailed blue coat, and light trousers. His look was rather stupid, but in reality he was wide awake."

There is no doubt that Balfour is at his best when he provides incisive sketches of some of the members of the R. & A. whom he especially respected. When he writes about them, we learn a good deal about him. For example, there was Sir Hope Grant, a career soldier and a gifted cellist. "I first met him in 1851, when he came home from the first Chinese war, and before the Indian Mutiny, where he distinguished himself so gallantly." There was George Glennie, "who was never excelled at any part of the game by a gentleman player, and whose modest bearing made him universally liked." There was "my dear old relative, Mr. Whyte-Melville, who, while he was never a fine player, was a capital partner, and was extremely fond of the game, and who played till he was past eighty-five—three days every week, and two rounds every day, in summer and winter, and in all weather." And there was Captain W.H. Maitland Dougall, who, in 1860, when a terrible storm forced the annual competition for the gold medal to be postponed, joined the crew of a lifeboat that was launched to go to the aid of a foundering vessel in St. Andrews Bay. Maitland Dougall took the stroke oar. "The men were rescued," Balfour recounts, "and the lifeboat came ashore in the afternoon. The play for the medal was begun after the rescue of the lifeboat. The wind was still furious. It was to Maitland Dougall's credit that, though his arms were sore, and he was stiff and all wet, he gained the Club gold medal at 112 strokes."

The man who turned in the lowest round on medal day at St. Andrews won the gold medal presented to the club by King William IV. The man who finished second won the gold medal awarded by the club. James Balfour, a very good golfer, never won the King William IV gold medal, but he won the club's gold medal three times—in 1853, 1857, and 1861. One year he shot a 93 in that competition, which would be the equivalent of breaking 70 today. In 1863 he was robbed of winning the club's gold medal a fourth time. As he tells the story, "Mr. Robert Clark, in playing the last hole home, lay near the road at one stroke fewer than I was. He played a pretty long stroke with his cleek and actually holed his ball, *thus tying with me for the medal! He gained the tie."*

That was hard luck, but when one thinks back on James Balfour and the zestful forty-five years he spent playing a then incomparable course with fellow members he admired and whose company he thoroughly enjoyed, one envies him and understands why he could not rest until he had got his reminiscences down on paper and had found the proper publisher.

One also understands why James Balfour became the head of a famous family of golfers. His son Leslie Balfour-Melville won the British Amateur in 1895, the same year as another son of his won the Australian Amateur. A lawyer by profession, Leslie Balfour-Melville was a tremendous all-around athlete. He won the Scottish lawn tennis championship. He also represented Scotland in rugby football and cricket. Before winning the British Amateur, he had reached the semi-finals twice—in 1888, when John Laidlay eliminated him, and in 1892, when John Ball eliminated him. In 1889, he reached the final but lost to Laidlay, 2 and 1. When he won the championship in 1895, he defeated Laurie Auchterlonie on the 19th hole in the semi-finals, and he then defeated the illustrious Ball on the 37th. Leslie Balfour-Melville was elected captain of the Royal & Ancient Golf Club of St. Andrews in 1906.

The Afterwords for this book and its companion selection, Horace G. Hutchinson's "Hints on the Game of Golf", have been kindly provided by Jack Nicklaus, the golfer most closely connected with St. Andrews over the last three decades. In the 1964 British Open, which was held at St. Andrews,

Nicklaus finished second to Tony Lema after playing a 66 and a 68 on the double round on Saturday. He won the 1970 British Open at St. Andrews after a thrilling playoff with Doug Sanders. When the Open was next held at St. Andrews in 1978, Nicklaus was again the winner, drawing away down the stretch from Simon Owen, of New Zealand. When Nicklaus returned to St. Andrews to play in the 1984 British Open, the University of St. Andrews awarded him the honorary degree of Doctor of Laws for his outstanding contributions as a player, a writer on golf, a golf-course architect, and for his many other personal contributions to the game he loves.

Herbert Warren Wind

REMINISCENCES

OF

GOLF

ON

ST. ANDREWS LINKS

BY

JAMES BALFOUR

EDINBURGH: DAVID DOUGLAS
1887

CONTENTS.

CHAPTER I.

LINKS.

HAVING played golf on these Links for somewhere about forty-five years, it has occurred to me to note for my own amusement some of the changes that have taken place during that time in this, one of the most fascinating of all athletic games.

The changes naturally resolve themselves into those on the Links—the Balls—the Clubs.

Before speaking of these, however, it may be well to mark the change of habits in the players during this generation. When I first visited St. Andrews there were only a few resident gentlemen who played, and some occasional strangers from a distance, from Musselburgh, Leith, and Perth. The custom then was to meet in the small Union Parlour in Golf Place about twelve o'clock, and arrange the matches. Parties at once proceeded to play, and if the match was finished two or three holes from home they immediately turned and played their second round, taking a glass of ginger beer at the fourth or "Ginger-beer" Hole. If, however, they finished their first round, they came into the Union Parlour only for ten minutes; did not sit down to lunch, but took very slight refreshment, and finished the second round a little after four. The dinner hour was then five.

How different now, when matches are made a week, or even a fortnight, in advance; when places are taken early in the morning, and a man is kept with a record to start each in his turn, and so prevent disputes about the order of play; when play is begun a little after nine, and fifty or sixty matches start between that hour and twelve; when parties have to wait a quarter of an hour for one another at the "high hole"; when an hour or an hour and a half is devoted to lunch, and the second rounds are not begun till between two and half-past three! The dinner hour is half-past seven, to give time to have a putting match on the Ladies' Links with the fair and enthusiastic devotees of the game!

The Links belong to Mr. Cheape, the proprietor of the neighbouring estate of Strathyrum. Their length is nearly two miles, and their breadth at the broadest part about $2\frac{2}{5}$ths of a mile. In some distant geological epoch they must have been submerged by the sea, but they are now protected from its waves by high natural embankments of sand. They were originally covered with thick whins, rough grass, heather, and bents. Out of this a golf-course was formed like a narrow ribbon in the form of a shepherd's crook, over which the public have acquired a servitude of playing golf. The course is marked off by march stones. The approximate distance of the holes from one another is as follows :—

	Yards.
No. 1, . . .	360
„ 2, . . .	450
„ 3, . . .	335
„ 4, . . .	375
„ 5, . . .	540
„ 6, . . .	370
„ 7, . . .	350
„ 8, . . .	150
„ 9, . . .	300
	3230
	2
	1760)6460(3 miles.
	5280
	1180

Or $3\frac{3}{4}$ miles.

The length of the course as the crow flies is

thus $3\frac{3}{4}$ miles; but following the ball in a zigzag way, the distance walked is generally considered to be about five miles. The course is marvellously adapted to the game. It used to be flanked by high whins for the greater part of its extent, and these formed an interesting hazard. The turf is smooth and fine; the subsoil is sandy; the surface sometimes undulating and sometimes flat. There are beautiful level putting-greens, while the course is studded with sand-pits, or bunkers, as golfers call them. These, with the ever-recurring hazards of whin, heather, and bent all combine to give endless variety, and to adapt the Links at St. Andrews for the game of golf in a way quite unsurpassed anywhere else. If there be added to its golfing charms the charms of all its surroundings—the grand history of St. Andrews and its sacred memories—its delightful air—the song of its numberless larks, which nestle among the whins—the scream of the sea-birds flying overhead—the blue sea dotted with a few fishing-boats—the noise of its waves—the bay of the Eden as seen from the high hole when the tide is full—the venerable towers and the broken outline of the ancient city; and in the distance the Forfarshire coast, with the range of the Sidlaws, and, further off, the Grampian Hills, it may be truly said that, probably, no portion of ground of the same size on the whole surface of the globe has afforded so much innocent enjoyment to so many people of all ages from two to eighty-nine, and during so many generations.

The changes that have taken place on the course during these forty-five years have been very considerable. First of all, the course is much wider. Formerly there was only one hole on each putting-green, and players played to the same hole both going out and coming in. The party first on the green had the right to finish the hole before the match from the opposite direction came up. This naturally kept the course narrow, but when players began to multiply it was found to be inconvenient, and now it would be impossible. To obviate this it was resolved to have two holes on each putting-green, one of them being played to on going out and the other on coming in; or rather there were two distinct putting-greens parallel to one another, and a hole in each. This was virtually making two courses all along the Links—one for playing out and the other for coming in; thus the breadth of the course for golfing was gradually increased, till now it is about two-thirds broader than it used to be. This was probably unavoidable, owing to the increased number of players, but it has taken away much of the interest of the game. The only other plan that was suggested was to extend the course round the other side of the Links, and thus make it a circular one; but this was very properly rejected. To that there are many objections. It would have made the course shorter; it would have abolished all the present holes on the homeward line, some of which are so charming in themselves, and full of associations; it would also have deprived parties of the pleasure of meeting their friends, and hearing how their matches were getting on. It is to be hoped that such a proposal will never be renewed.

Let us now consider the changes that have taken place on each of the holes individually, and we shall do so by following the medal round, taking the course out by the right.

1. The first hole used always to be on the green beside the road. Its hazards were the road across the Links, the burn, the bunker on one side of the putting-green, as well as the turnpike road on the other—making thus a limited green with a narrow approach to it flanked by severe hazards.

The first hole on the medal round now is quite different. It is placed just beyond the burn, on a flat, smooth, broad green to the right of the course. The only hazards in the hole are the road across the

Links and the burn. There are none whatever close to the hole.

2. The tee for the second hole used to be, of course, near the road. There was then no separate teeing-grounds, but the rule was to tee within eight club-lengths of the hole. The ground between the wall and the bunkers towards the corner of the dyke, which is now often preferred as the shortest approach to the hole, was covered with thick whins, and was then quite unplayable. Consequently players were obliged to cross the course, and approach the hole by the right of the bunkers. The whins on the right made the course narrow in that direction, and the low ground to the right of the putting-green could not be played on on account of whins and rough grass, so that the hole was much more difficult both in playing and approaching than now. The putting-green, too, which was formerly on a slope, has been made quite level.

At present the tee of this hole is on the right of the Links, while the whins having been driven back, and the low ground to the right near the hole made quite playable, the hole can be played without any bunkers intervening, or any hazards of any kind. Of course if the player goes off the line he has to encounter some hazards. The putting-green, as has been said, is now on a flat and not a slope.

3. There used to be a thick bank of whins all along the left of the course by the side of the present railway, and the whins and rough grass on the right made it necessary to play straight in the centre, where was the Principal's Nose, with its little satellite of "Tam's Coo" (now filled up). The smaller bunker too, short of these, presented together with them dangerous traps. There was very little room indeed to pass them on either side. The hole was always in the *centre of the green*, so that the bunker which crosses the Links beside it had to be played over, else a considerable distance was lost by going to the right or left of it.

The tee is now on the right side of the green, and the ball from it is easily played to the right of the Principal's Nose, while the hole being to the right of the putting-green, it is readily approached without crossing the bunker.

4. Formerly the whins encroached so much on either side that it was necessary that the tee stroke should be played on or over the table in front of the tee, and then a very narrow course was left up to the hole, which was on a narrower putting-green than now, and it was usually placed nearer the bunkers.

The whins having been now driven back, the ball can be played to the right of the table. The course is clear for the second stroke, and the hole is placed to the right, far from the bunkers.

5. This hole is more altered than any other on the Links, and sadly destroyed. The tee stroke used always to be played to the right of the big bunker with the uncouth name, unless when now and then some huge driver "swiped over h— at one immortal go." The second stroke was always to the left on to the Elysian Fields, where the grass was then short and smooth like a putting-green. The third had to navigate the intricate "Beardies," and the fourth was across a wide, staring, horrid bunker, beyond which was a beautiful putting-green. Altogether, this used to be the finest golfing hole, certainly on the Links, and probably in the world. There were beautiful lies when the play was correct, very difficult hazards, and a perfect putting-green.

Now the play is quite different. The Elysian Fields are avoided, and the hole is played on a lower level, where high whins formerly grew, which made play there impossible. There is hardly any hazard; there are no bunkers of any consideration, and the approach to the green is a blind stroke without any bunker between. The hole is altogether much tamer, and less interesting, as well as easier. The young laird of the Links would do the game of golf an unspeakable benefit if he would plough up the low course, or honeycomb it with bunkers, so as to compel players to return to the old line on the Elysian Fields.

6. The sixth hole is also much altered. It used to be one of the most dangerous on the Links, but two or three large and important bunkers have been filled up to make a double course. This reduces the number of hazards materially, and the whins have so much disappeared that it is safe to go round the bunkers, playing well to the right, instead of being compelled to play over them. The putting-green, too, is greatly changed. Formerly it had no turf, but was merely earth, heather, and shells, from which it got its name of the heather hole, or the "hole o' shell," but it has now been turfed, and, like the other greens, is carefully kept.

7. The course here was a narrow one, so that the first stroke was necessarily played over—very often, unfortunately, into—the bunker that crosses the green; but there was not much room to go on either side of it. The putting-green at the high hole, which was always placed near the Eden, was then surrounded with thick, bent grass, leaving a very limited space near the hole. Besides, the ground was sandy and soft. The deterioration of this putting-green has been averted by the growth of rank sea-grass on the banks of the Eden, which

prevents the sand from being blown on to the Links. These bents were a serious hazard.

8. The short hole is not much changed, except that the putting-green is wider than it used to be.

9, or last hole going out, used to be principally heather, but a large portion of that heather was some years ago taken up and relaid with turf. The putting-green is now also much broader than formerly.

Having now reached the end hole, let us retrace our way and compare the holes going home as they now are with what they used to be. This may be thought to be unnecessary, as exactly the same ground has to be travelled over as has been already described. This is quite a mistake. Although the ground is the same, the various holes are as different as if they were on different Links.

1. The principal difference on the first hole home is that the course was formerly narrower, and the heather has been replaced by turf. If a ball was at all drawn to the left, it used to be either lost in the whins or so imbedded among them that it had to be played out at the sacrifice of at least one stroke, if not more; but now it often lies very tolerably even there, and can be played forward. Near the hole, too, the ground short of it and to the left was

so covered with thick grass that if a ball got there it had an exceedingly bad lie. Now the ball has a fair lie where the grass used to be so heavy.

2. The short hole home is not much changed, except that the bents have disappeared, as already stated, while the putting-green is much harder and broader.

3. In driving this hole there is now plenty of room to pass the bunker that crosses the green on either side of it. The rough ground at both ends of the putting-green has disappeared, and the putting-green itself has been turfed, and is no longer shelly.

4. The next hole used to be one of the most difficult on the Links, and more medals have been lost at it than at any other. It has a good many hazards yet, but two of the largest bunkers have been filled up to make a course to the left, as well as one to the right. In former times Allan Robertson used to play the first stroke often with the short spoon short of all the bunkers, and the second with the short spoon over the bunkers, and the third from behind the hill with the short spoon also, on to the green. Now there is plenty of room to avoid the bunkers, both on the right and left: players can have a long stroke off the tee, while long drivers may be on the green in two, and some of the worst bunkers not played over at all.

5. The long hole home, like the long hole out, has been entirely changed. The big yawning bunker in front of the tee, that was ready to catch a topped ball and to hold it, is almost entirely avoided, while the "Beardies," where so many balls used to be kidnapped, and from which escape was not always made with the loss of only one stroke, are never looked at.

Now the play is on the low ground to the left of the Elysian Fields, thus crossing the bunker diagonally. This line used to be absolutely impossible. There are now no hazards there, or only trifling ones. The hole itself is always placed on the right or left of the putting-green instead of the centre, just between two bunkers, the approach to which used to be at the sacrifice of some distance to circumvent the bunkers.

6. The whins on the left, where the first stroke was played, protruded far on to the Links, and the ball was either caught in them or had to be played right in the centre. There was no possible play to the left of the table, and the second stroke had to go straight over that table; if that stroke were at all short, the ground, which sloped down towards dangerous bunkers, drew the ball into them. Now the hole can be played to the left or right without much risk.

7. Formerly, there was little room to pass the "Principal's Nose" on either side from the tee,

and it, and "Tammy's Coo" beside it, were ugly hazards. The line of whins alongside the present railway was an additional difficulty if the right-hand course was adopted; and if the left, the ground which is now clear was then impracticable from whins. The putting-green itself, as has been mentioned before, has been levelled, so that the hole, instead of being on a slope as formerly, is now on a flat table, and the low ground to the left of it is no longer covered with whins.

8. Playing off from the hole at the dyke, the ground in front is now cleared of the dense clump of whins that used to be immediately in front of the tee. There has been no other alteration on this hole of great consequence, except that the grass, which is sometimes long and heavy after much rain, is mowed with a scythe, and a large bank of rushes has been removed.

9. The principal difference on the last hole is on the putting-green. That has been quite changed by the formation of an artificial table-land, which forms a beautiful green. Formerly the hole was on broken ground in a hollow, with the ground sloping down on both sides. Shortly before my time, there was another serious hazard made by the sea, which came up to the stair of the present Club-House.

That hazard was a very serious one, as the sand at that place was as deep as at the high hole. The last hole being often placed near the edge of the green was close to the sand. But the Links have now been made much wider by the rubbish from the town having reclaimed a large portion from the sea, and there are no hazards on that side.

Having now gone over the golf-course both going out and coming in, it only remains further to say on this head that the Links are far more carefully kept than they used to be. Tom Morris superintends this with great assiduity, and he has two men under him who are constantly employed in keeping the bunkers at the proper size, in filling up rabbit-scrapes or other holes, and in returfing places which have given way. The putting-greens also, instead of being left in their natural state as formerly, are now carefully rolled with a heavy roller, — mowed with a machine,—and watered in dry weather from a well that has been sunk near each of them. The putting is made smoother and better, and much truer.

A separate teeing-ground has also been provided at each hole, which preserves the putting-greens from being broken by the tee strokes. A wooden box filled with sand for the tee, and placed at the teeing-ground, is a novelty and an additional refinement.

CHAPTER II.

BALLS AND CLUBS.

Balls.

LET us now turn to the changes that have taken place on the Balls. Forty years ago, and indeed from time immemorial, the only kind of ball with which golf had been played was made of leather stuffed with feathers till it was as hard as gutta percha. In making it the leather was cut into three pieces, softened with alum and water, and sewed together by waxed thread, while a small hole was left for putting in the feathers, which was done with a strong stuffing-iron.

The hole in the leather, which did not affect the flight of the ball, but slightly interfered with its putting quality, was then sewed up, and the ball received three coats of paint. A man could make only four balls in a day. They were thus scarce and expensive, and were not round, but rather oblong. The only ball-maker at St. Andrews was Allan Robertson. The trade was hereditary in his family, as both father and grandfather had likewise been ball-makers.

He was assisted by Tom Morris and Lang Willie. They worked together in Allan's kitchen, and the balls were sold at the window at the back of his house, at the corner of the Links and Golf Place. Allan charged 1s. 8d. a ball, or £1 a dozen. Gourlay of Musselburgh charged 2s. for each of his. These balls did not last long, perhaps not more than one round. They opened at the seams, especially in wet weather. Indeed, whenever the seam of a ball was cut by the club, the ball burst, and became useless. This very frequently happened, insomuch that the caddies generally took out six or eight balls with them.

About the beginning of the year 1848 balls were first made of gutta percha. I remember the commencement of them perfectly. My brother-in-law, Admiral Maitland Dougall, played a double match at Blackheath with the late Sir Ralph Anstruther and William Adam of Blair-Adam and another friend with gutta-percha balls on a very wet day. They afterwards dined together at Sir Charles Adam's at Greenwich Hospital, and Sir Ralph said after dinner: "A most curious thing—here is a golf ball of gutta percha; Maitland and I have played with it all day in the rain, and it flies better at the end of the day than it did at the beginning." Maitland came to Edinburgh immediately after and told me of this. We at once wrote to London for some of these balls, and went to Musselburgh to try them. Gourlay the ball-maker had heard of them, and followed us a round. He was astonished to see how they flew, and, being round, how they rolled straight to the hole on the putting-green. He was alarmed for his craft, and having an order from Sir David Baird to send him some balls whenever he had a supply by him, he forwarded to him that evening six dozen! Sir David accordingly was one of the last who adhered to the feather balls, and did not acknowledge the superiority of the others until his large supply was finished. At first they were made with the hand by rolling them on a flat board; thus made, they were round and smooth. They were not painted, but used with their natural brown colour. When new, they did not fly well, but ducked in the air. To remedy this they were hammered with a heavy hammer, but this did not effect the object. They still ducked until they got some rough usage from the cleek or iron. This made cuts on their sides, which were not liked; but it made them fly. These cuts were easily removed by dipping them in hot water at night. I remember once playing with old Philp, the club-maker (who, by the way, was no contemptible player). I had a gutta ball, and he had a feather one. With the dislike which all the tradesmen then had for the former, he said, "Do you play with these putty balls?" "Yes," I answered. "But does not the cleek cut them?" "O yes," I said, "but if you give them a hot bath at night that puts them all right." "That 's the mischief o't," he replied. Yet it was soon found out that this same hot bath, while it cured the wound, spoiled the ball. I remember an amusing proof of this. I and a friend on the day before the medal played with two guttas, and they worked beautifully, so that we resolved to play with them next day for the medal. But as they had been a good deal hacked, we dipped them in hot water over-night, and removed these defects. When, however, we played off the tee next day before an assembled crowd, among whom were the ball and club-makers, both the balls whirred and ducked amid the chuckling and jeering and loud laughter of the onlookers; we had to put down feather balls next hole. The fact was, they required these indentations to make them fly. About this time it occurred to an ingenious saddler in South Street to hammer them all round with the thin or sharp end of the hammer. The experiment was completely successful, and the ball thus hammered came rapidly into use, and they were soon improved by being painted. But the ball-makers were still bitterly opposed to them, as they threatened to destroy their trade,[1] and both Allan and Tom resolved that they would never play in a match where these balls were used. In an unlucky hour, however, Tom good-naturedly broke his pledge, and played with a gentleman as his partner who had gutta balls. When Allan discovered it he was much annoyed with Tom. Tom, when he saw this, gave up his employment under him, and opened a shop of his own, where he made both kinds of balls, and also clubs. Allan in a little time followed suit with the balls, as he discovered that he could make a dozen guttas in a shorter time than he could make one feather ball, and the sale of them increased prodigiously. After that an iron mould was invented for making these balls, and on being taken from the mould, they were indented with the thin end of the hammer. But latterly the moulds have the indentations in them, so that the ball is now produced indented and ready for being painted. The balls are made everywhere now, but some are better than others, probably because the maker takes greater pains to use good gutta percha.

[1] No wonder, as there were 2456 balls turned out by Allan Robertson in 1844.

Various modifications of this ball have been tried, but without success. Lately, however, another kind has been played with, called the *Eclipse.* It is not exactly known how it is made, but it is supposed to be a composition of gutta percha and vulcanised india-rubber and cork. It is a little softer than the gutta-percha ball, it makes no click when struck by the club, while the irons make no mark on it, nor does it ever lose its shape. It is a moot point whether it or the gutta-percha ball is the best, and some of the finest players differ as to that. The professionals generally prefer the gutta. Those who like the Eclipse claim for it that it holds the wind better; it runs better, especially if the ground is hard either from frost or drought; and they think it is more to be depended on in putting. On the other hand, those who prefer the guttas say that, if they do not run so far as the others, they fly further; that they require less physical force, as they spring with greater elasticity from the club; that they are more easily picked up and dropped near the hole at the approach stroke. They maintain, too, that they put as well as the others, and they like to hear the click in striking, to which they have been accustomed. But whatever be the comparative merits of the two balls, it is not improbable that the

Eclipse will be the ball of the future, unless something else is invented. They last much longer, and so are a good deal cheaper than the guttas. For this reason boys naturally play with them. They will get accustomed to them in their youth, and will continue to play with them when they become men.

Clubs.

The change in the Clubs has not been so important as on the Balls, but some have been discontinued that were formerly used, and others have been introduced. For example, the driving putter is never now played with. It was a club with a putter head, but with a flatter angle than a putter, a shaft about the length of a middle spoon, and, though stiff, had a spring in it. It was used to play out of bents and thick grass, but as these have now disappeared, so has the club. It was convenient, too, for playing against wind.

Another club that I fear is fast getting obsolete is the Baffing Spoon. As golfers know, to baff a ball is to touch the turf below the ball pretty firmly when it is struck, and the ball is thus raised into the air. The Baffy is a very short spoon, about the length of a putter, but spooned twice the depth of an ordinary short spoon. It is used when near the hole, and when the ball has to be lifted over a hazard or uneven ground. There are few prettier strokes in the game. The ball is tossed high in the air, and hovers for a moment, as if to choose what blade of grass to alight on, then drops, and does not run above a foot or so. It is not only a pretty stroke, but a very effective one when well played. In the hands of Captain Dalgleish, Sir David Baird, Shihallion, or Sir Robert Hay, the Baffy was a wonderful weapon. But now men have grown so fond of cleeks and irons in all shapes and sizes that it is despised. It is said that Allan Robertson introduced the use of the cleek when near the hole. If so, it is, I think, a pity that he did. It is not so pretty a stroke; it destroys the green, as some even intentionally cut the turf with it; and it is not more sure than the stroke with the "Baffy."

While these two clubs have gone out of fashion, two others have been introduced. One is the Iron Niblick, with which to play out of bunkers, or when in a hole or cart-rut. It is a heavy iron, with a short round head, and is admirably adapted for bunkers, as it takes much less sand than the ordinary heavy iron with which that stroke used to be played.

The other new club is the Wooden Niblick. It is a

long spoon, with a very short head, plated with brass on the bottom, from which it gets its other name of the "Brassy." It is used for playing a cupped or bad-lying ball, or a ball on a road. On a road the brass bottom saves the club from being destroyed by the hard metal, or turned so easily as a wooden one would be. It is extremely useful, and with its short head many men can play a cupped ball as well as a ball from the tee with a play-club. No set would be complete without having both an Iron Niblick and a Brassy.[1]

[1] I have read these two chapters to Tom Morris, and he indorses every word of them.

CHAPTER III.

MEDALS.

THE first prize played for by the Club was a silver club, the winner of which was to be Captain for the year, and was to attach to it a silver ball, with his name and the date of his having won the club. It was first played for in 1754, and has been regularly the Captain's prize ever since, so that it is now covered with medals. These are treated with great reverence, as all new members are required to kiss them at the first dinner which he attends after his election.

This prize was competed for in the ordinary way for many years; but by and by the Club came to be of opinion that the Captain, instead of being only distinguished as a first-class golfer, should rather be a gentleman of good social position who took an interest in the game, his principal duties being to preside at the dinners and ball, and to represent the Club in society. It was accordingly agreed that, while he should be Captain in virtue of winning the silver club, some one should be selected by the old Captains, against whom no other member should play. This plan has been long acted on, the gentleman selected playing only one stroke, when he is declared winner of the club.

In 1833 Mr. Whyte-Melville presented the Club with a silver putter, on the understanding that, although no balls were to be appended to it, the gold medals of the Club should be attached, so that, as the silver club handed down to posterity the names of those who had presided over its meetings, the putter might transmit in a similar manner the medals bearing the names of those members who had signalised themselves by their superiority at play in the game of golf.

On the system of selection, a great number of noblemen and gentlemen have been Captains. In the year 1864 the Prince of Wales was nominated as Captain, but as His Royal Highness could not be present, both his play and duties as Captain were done by proxy. But in 1875 the late Prince Leopold, Duke of Albany, was selected, and he was good enough to come to St. Andrews for the purpose. There was great excitement in the prospect of his visit. The day before the medal was wet and gloomy, but immediately after breakfast on the medal day it cleared up, and the weather became charming. The Prince stayed at Mount Melville. While driving in in the morning, he saw St. Andrews gay with flags at every available place—so gay that the ancient city hardly knew itself. On appearing on the Links, a great concourse of spectators had assembled to see His Royal Highness play for the club. A rope was stretched out to prevent the people from crowding upon him. Tom Morris teed his ball, and the Prince, evidently a little nervous lest he should top it, struck a good, clean, long stroke over the heads of the people, amid much cheering. He was then declared winner of the club, which was proclaimed, as usual, by the firing of the cannon. The gold medals were afterwards competed for, forty-seven couples joining in the contest. His Royal Highness followed some of the favourite players, and watched the game. In the evening he presided at the dinner, where he presented the medals with his usual gracious and affable manner. He also gave a handsome silver medal of his own to the winner of William the Fourth's medal, to be retained by him as a memorial of his being Captain. He presided at the ball next evening, when, by his whole bearing there, as well as during all his visit to St. Andrews, he won the hearts of every one. Nowhere were the tidings of his early death in 1884 received with more real sorrow.

It may be mentioned that the uniform worn by the Captain in the evening, both at the dinner and ball, as well as the former Captains, is a red dress coat, with blue collar, and gilt buttons, stamped with a St. Andrew's cross. The uniform of the members of the Club on the Links is a red jacket, with blue collar, and gilt buttons with the St. Andrew's cross. At one time it was compulsory on members to wear their uniform when playing, under penalty of a fine. But when it became customary for gentlemen to wear shooting-coats in the forenoon, the rule was not enforced, and the uniform is now not always used.

After the arrangement by which the Captain was to be virtually elected, the Club gave a gold medal, to be competed for once a year. It was to be gained by the member who did a round of the Links in the fewest number of strokes. Any two members can play against each other as they may arrange, and the order in which they start is fixed by ballot on the previous day. This medal was first played for in 1806, and it continued to be the principal golfing prize until the year 1837, when His Majesty King

William the Fourth—who had in 1834 become patron of the Club, and authorised it to be styled "The Royal and Ancient Golf Club of St. Andrews"—presented the Club with a handsome gold medal, to be played for annually. This medal from that year became the first prize of the Club, and the second was the Club gold medal. They are both competed for on the same day in autumn—generally the last Wednesday of September.

In 1838 the Queen-Dowager graciously presented the Club with a gold medal, called the Royal Adelaide Medal, which was to be worn by the Captain during his term of office.

Besides these gold medals, Major Belches of Invermay in 1836 presented the Club with a "silver cross of St. Andrew's;" and in 1846 the Bombay Club presented it with a silver medal. These silver prizes are competed for at the spring meeting of the Club—generally on the first Wednesday of May—on the same terms and in the same way as the other prizes are played for in autumn.

In 1881 the Royal Blackheath Golf Club presented to the Royal and Ancient Golf Club of St. Andrews a gold medal, in honour of Mr. George Glennie, who was a respected member of both Clubs. It is competed for both in May and October, and is gained by the player whose combined scores at the spring and autumn meetings are the lowest.

The only handicap prize in the Club is a handsome cup, which was presented by the Calcutta Golf Club, and was played for in 1885 for the first time. It is decided, not by strokes, but by holes, the various players receiving odds from those that are fixed as the scratch.

Captain Daniel Stewart, the Captain of the Club for last year (1886), presented a silver jug to the player who should do the last nine holes when playing for the medal in the fewest strokes, and who should not gain either of the medals. The idea was that any player who had been unfortunate in going out might be encouraged still to keep up his interest in the game to the close. The jug was not a challenge prize, but was to be retained by the winner.

All these prizes, except Prince Albert's and Captain Stewart's, are challenge prizes, to be held only for a year; but the winners of the gold medals in autumn and the silver prizes in spring each receive a small medal, in gold and silver respectively, to be retained by them, and worn on the coat.

CHAPTER IV.

PLAYERS.

Now let me indulge myself by recalling the memory of some of those who are gone, with whom I have often played. Among all the great variety of persons with whom I have joined in the game, Sir Hope Grant was my most constant opponent. He was a charming companion and fast friend, a perfect gentleman both in feeling and manner, a distinguished and eminent soldier, a graceful rider, and an excellent player on the violoncello, of which he was passionately fond. He was also one of the keenest golfers I ever knew, and I have known few who played better. He drove long, low balls, held his cleek short, played it from the knee, and when he was in form was a very good putter, always using a wooden club, which he held short. I first met him in 1851, when he came home from the first Chinese war, and before the Indian Mutiny, where he distinguished himself so gallantly. His friends crowded round him at the Union Parlour. They knew what a fine player he had been, and that he used to play matches for £100 with John Wood, the best gentleman player then, or perhaps that ever was, at Musselburgh. A match was made up for him, in which I happened to be one of the players. Before starting, Sir Hugh Playfair, who was not playing, said, "You know, Hope, I don't bet much, but I will go half a sovereign on this match with you." Sir Hugh did not know what an entire change had come over Sir Hope's religious principles during his residence in India and China, and which involved a change of practice; but Sir Hope (or Colonel Grant, as he then was) at once answered, "Oh, I forgot to tell you all that I have given up that sort of thing, and I now play for nothing." "Go half a crown," said Sir Hugh. "No, nothing." "A something—a fiddle-string." "No, nothing." He was delighted to find that I acted on the same principle, and never betted, believing that the game was in itself sufficiently interesting without adding to it the gambler's excitement. From that hour began a fast friendship between us, which never had a check till he died in 1875. When he died Sir Stafford Northcote said of him very truly in the House of Commons, of which he was then the leader, "His modesty was equal to his courage." And there were his two brothers—John Grant of Kilgraston, and Sir Francis, President of the Royal Academy. They were not great golfers, but very fond of it, and were both excellent company. Sir Hugh Playfair's name will be long remembered and his influence felt in St. Andrews. He inaugurated the Union Parlour, where the entry-money was £1 and the annual subscription 5s. He also commenced the present Club House, which has grown into such comfortable proportions. The entry-money now is £8, and the annual subscription £3. The membership is 870. Then there was his brother-in-law, Captain Archie Dalgleish, once the cock of the green. These two used to take up all strangers coming to St. Andrews, and were seldom beaten. There was also Captain Campbell, familiarly called Shihallion, and Saddell (another Campbell), magnificent and pompous, and Sir Thomas Moncrieffe, with a lively, pleasing manner; Sir Robert Hay, who was tall and handsome, with an elegant style of play; Sir Ralph Anstruther and his brother, afterwards Colonel Lloyd Anstruther, with the former's popular son Sir Robert; and George Whyte-Melville the novelist—witty, agreeable, and kindly, full of racy anecdotes in the Club between rounds; George Glennie, who was never excelled at any part of the game by a gentleman player, and whose modest bearing made him universally liked. Then there was Sir John Low of Clatto, who long held high appointments in India, and whose manners were cultured by associating with princes and statesmen; his excellent brother, the Colonel; my old schoolfellow, Goddard, whose beautiful style was modelled on that of John H. Wood, of whom it has been said that it was a study in the fine arts to see John Wood strike a ball. There was also J. O. Fairlie of Coodham, well known on the race-course and in the hunting-field, but a keen golfer, and a first-class player. Having learned the game rather late in life, his style was not graceful. He played with his whole body rather than with his arms, but he drove well, and was very sure. His manner was quiet and still; when playing important matches he was always silent. I once tied with him for William the Fourth's medal, and in playing off the tie he never uttered a single word during the whole round, not even in answer to an observation.

There are others yet alive, whom I forbear to name, but I must not forget my dear old relative, Mr. Whyte-Melville, who, while he never was a fine player, was a capital partner, and was extremely fond of the game, and who played till he was past eighty-five—three days every week, and two rounds every day, in summer and winter, and in all weathers—wind, rain, snow, or sunshine. On his death-bed he asked me to take a set of his clubs as a memorial of the many pleasant matches we had had together. I felt it to be kind and touching. He was deservedly popular. He and Lady Catherine dispensed profuse hospitality at their family seat of Mount Melville, about three miles from St. Andrews. When he was about 77, the Club asked him to allow his picture to be painted, that it might be placed in the Club House. It is a full-length portrait, by his old friend Frank Grant—one of the last and one of the best of his portraits. It is not only a good likeness, but an excellent golfing picture. He is represented as having finished the first hole at the road going out. His putter is still in his hand. His caddie is teeing his ball, while his play club is lying on the ground ready to be handed to him. The ancient stone bridge over the burn is shown—once the only bridge across the burn, and which has been traversed homeward by many an anxious foot when the match was all even and one to play; the Club House is in the distance, with the Martyrs' Monument. The only other portrait in the Club is that of Sir Hugh Playfair.

The late Lord Eglinton was a keen player at this, as at most other athletic sports. He was at St. Andrews in October 1861, and on the day before the medal the weather was beautiful. He played three rounds with Mr. Grant of Kilgraston, Sir Francis Grant, and Mr. Little Gilmour. After Sir Hope and I had finished our match, he asked me to go out a few holes and walk in with his brothers and Lord Eglinton. We did so; his lordship was enjoying himself extremely. He expressed his delight with the scenery at the high hole—and indeed he frequently admired the whole landscape, as the descending sun lengthened our shadows on that October afternoon. He afterwards went out to Mount Melville to dinner. When coming away in the evening he complained to a friend, as they were passing through the library, that he had felt rather unwell in the drawing-room, but that he was now all right. When, however, he got to the hall, while the butler was helping him on with his great-coat, he fell down in a fit of apoplexy, was carried to a bedroom, never spoke again, and died two days after. As may be supposed, this cast a sad gloom over the gathering for the medal next day, all the more that on the same day another well-known member of the Club, Mr. Guthrie of Craigie, had a stroke of apoplexy in the billiard-room; but he recovered, and lived for some years.

Mr. Stuart Grace, though not himself a golfer, having been the indefatigable Secretary of the Club since 1842 till 1885—that is, ever since I was a member of it,—I must not omit to mention. It is rather remarkable that four generations of Mr. Grace's family have been Secretaries of the Club. His grandfather was Secretary for thirty years; his father for twenty-four years, and himself for forty-three years; his son has now been elected as his successor. The three first members of the family were honorary Secretaries. At the close of the late Mr. Grace's tenure of office, the Club presented him with a service of plate; Mr. Stuart Grace, who has recently retired, has also been presented with silver plate, which he has well deserved for the attention which he has paid to the business of the Club for so long a period, and for the courtesy which he has invariably shown to all its members.

CHAPTER V.

PROFESSIONALS AND CADDIES.

Of club-makers, no man has ever approached Hugh Philp, and even now to possess a club of his is a treasure like an old Cremona violin to a musician, or a Toledo blade to a swordsman. He was a quiet and thoroughly respectable man, had a fine eye for a club, with exquisite taste, while he was simple and natural in his manner. His assistant, James Wilson, who worked with him for many years, and after his death opened an establishment of his own, was also much liked.

Let me recall some of the professionals and the old caddies. First among these was Allan Robertson, the prince of golfers. He and his father and grandfather had been ball-makers, when feather balls were the only balls, for more than a hundred years. He was a short, little, active man, with a pleasant face, small features, and a merry twinkle in his eye. He was universally popular, not a bit forward, but withal easy and full of self-respect. He generally wore a red, round jacket, and played constantly with gentlemen, both in matches of great importance, and in those that were only more or less important. His style was neat and effective. He held his clubs near the end of the handle, even his putter high up. His clubs were light, and his stroke an easy, swift switch. With him the game was one as much of head as of hand. He always kept cool, and generally pulled through a match even when he got behind. He was a natural gentleman, honourable and true. He died of jaundice on 1st September 1859, when only about the age of forty-four, much regretted.

Next to him was Tom Morris, now called "Old Tom." He began by helping Allan to make balls, and was very nearly his match at the game. His style I need not describe, as all golfers of the present generation know it. He still flourishes on the Links, and is still a fine player. He and Allan were together the champions of their day. Tom has always been respected, not only as a player, but for his excellent private character. There is an anecdote told of him, which I have great pleasure in repeating, because it is so honourable to him. On one occasion he was playing with the late Captain Broughton, and when at the high hole Tom's ball was lying in the bents that used then to surround it, the Captain said, "O Tom, you had better give up the hole; you are playing three more, and you are in the bents." "No," said Tom; "I'll perhaps hole this." "I'll give you £50 if you do." "Done with you, Captain," said Tom, and he holed it! Next morning the Captain brought £50, and handed it to him. "What is that?" said Tom. "What you won yesterday." "Take it away," exclaimed Tom, "I would not touch it. We were both in fun." This was exceedingly creditable to Tom, and showed real good feeling. If he had taken it, no one could have found fault with him, and £50 offered to a tradesman was a temptation. I had often heard the story from Campbell of Saddel, who was present, and other gentlemen, but I once asked Tom himself about it. He said it was all true, and he laughingly added, "You should have seen the Captain's face when I went in!" Tom, as is well known, is now the Conservator of the Links, and has a large establishment for making both clubs and balls.

His son, "Young Tommy," was perhaps the best player that ever appeared on the green. He was a tall, handsome athlete, and unmatched at all parts of the game. His victorious career began in 1867, when he was sixteen. It continued without a break till his early death in 1875. During these eight years he exhibited as remarkable a display of golf as has ever been seen. When he died, at the early age of twenty-four, he was buried in the ground at the old Cathedral, where a monument has been erected to his memory by contributions from sixty golfing clubs.

Among the older professionals were the twin brothers Dunn of Musselburgh. They were beautiful golfers, and fought many pitched battles with Allan and Tom. They ran them hard, but could not beat them.

Referring to the caddies, there were Sandy Pirie, who carried for Sir Hope Grant, and Sandy Herd, who carried first for Saddell and afterwards for Mr. Whyte-Melville; Charlie Thomson, once a crack player, as most of the others were; and many other most respectable men. But perhaps the greatest character among them was "Lang Willie." He was very tall, about six feet two, with bent knees and a slouching gait, a tall hat, swallow-tailed blue coat, and light trousers. His look was rather stupid, but he was in reality wide awake. He used to insist that he drank nothing but sweet milk, greatly to Allan's amusement, who knew better. He was much taken out as an instructor of beginners, and when one met him and asked him how his pupil was getting on, he had always the same stereotyped answer, "Jist surprisin'," which might mean either very well or very ill. On one occasion he was teaching one of the Professors of the University the noble game. But the said Professor was not a promising pupil. As he hammered away, sometimes "missing the globe," sometimes topping the ball, or cutting up large divots of turf, Willie fairly got out of patience, and said to him, "You see, Professor, as long as ye are learning thae lads at College Latin and Greek it is easy work, but when ye come to play golf ye maun hae a heid!" On another occasion he was carrying in a match, when, at the last hole coming home, the party had to wait till a young man on horseback had passed along the road. The rider was not very steady in his saddle, and Willie quietly remarked, "I think that lad is a wee lowse in the glue"—a phrase which golfers will understand who have felt the inconvenience of their club-head getting rather loose. Willie had more than one stroke of paralysis. I could not help being amused at his description of the first one. I asked him one day what he had felt. He said he felt nothing, but in the morning his sister said to him that his face was twisted. "I said to her, 'Nonsense, lassie,' but when I sat down to my parritch my jaw wouldna work!" At last he was overtaken by a fit on the Links, was carried home in an omnibus, and died in about twenty minutes after.

CHAPTER VI.

INCIDENTS IN GOLF.

FROM what has been said as to the changes in the Links, the Balls, and the Clubs, it is obvious that the round ought to be done in much fewer strokes now than formerly. How many fewer it is not easy accurately to determine. Some say twenty. I incline to think fifteen or sixteen, but I believe that every year it will be done in fewer for some little time, as the course gets broader and the hazards fewer. The best gauge, perhaps, is the score at which the medal has been gained from time to time. In the Appendix will be found the number of strokes that all the medals have been gained at since 1806, the furthest back year of which a record has been kept. From this list it will be seen that before the introduction of gutta percha, and the change of making two putting-greens at each hole, the lowest figure at which the medal was gained was in 1834, when it was taken at 97 by Mr. Robert Oliphant, while in 1839 Mr. Andrew Stirling and Mr. John H. Wood of Leith tied for it at 99; but these were exceptionally low; at that time it was reckoned to be very good if the medal was won at 103 or 104.

The fall has since been gradual, thus proving that it is not so much, at least, the superiority of the players now, but the comparative ease of the game. Young players are apt to think that the play is superior to what it used to be, but old men doubt this. They admit that the first-class players are more numerous than they formerly were, but they think that is because the game is played by a greater number. They maintain that there were formerly a few as good players as any of the present generation. The proportion is probably nearly the same.

After the introduction of gutta-percha balls, but before the change of the greens, the numbers fell to 98, 97, 96, at which last figure the silver cross was gained in the spring of 1850 by Mr. George Condie, and in 1852 Captain Maitland Dougall, and in 1853 Mr. Jelf Sharpe, each gained the same prize at the same figure—96. But the autumn medal had never been gained under 97. I have a vivid recollection of the autumn of the year 1850, when King William the Fourth's medal was played for. The Club was then just a hundred years old. The late Earl of Eglinton was Captain. There was a large turn-out both of players and spectators; most, if not all, of the best players of the day were present. The weather was lovely. One of the most successful medal-players of his time, now Admiral Maitland Dougall, who had gained the silver cross at 96 the year before, came in early in the day at 95, and was congratulated by every one on being sure to be the winner, and at a stroke lower than any medal had ever been gained during a hundred years before. But a little later in the day I was fortunate enough to come in at 93, and still later, to my mortification, Captain Stewart came in in 90, he thus winning the first medal, and I the second. It may be interesting to see some of the scores on that day. They were as follows:—

Captain Stewart, . . .	90
Mr. Balfour, ...	93
Captain Maitland Dougall, . .	95
Mr. George Condie, . . .	96
Mr. Goddard, ...	96
Mr. Glennie, ...	98
Mr. P. Alexander, . . .	99
Mr. Campbell of Saddel, . .	100
Mr. Ord Campbell, . . .	100
Sir Thomas Moncrieffe, . .	102

Bets were taken that the medals would never be won in 90 and 93 again. But they were. Shortly after the double holes with the double course were introduced, when the score began to fall more decidedly, insomuch that in the spring of 1883 the silver cross was gained by Mr. Alexander Stuart at 83, the lowest that it has yet reached, and in the autumn of 1886 King William the Fourth's medal was gained by Mr. S. M. Ferguson at 84, the lowest score for that medal.

Looking over the list of medal-holders, it will be observed that in the history of the Club the first gold medal has been gained for three years in succession by only two members, viz., Mr. Robert Patullo in 1812-13-14, and Mr. Leslie M. Balfour in 1875-76-77. Mr. George Glennie gained the King William the Fourth medal in 1855, at 88, before there were double holes, a figure which was never equalled till 1879, twenty-four years afterwards, when Mr. Charles Anderson gained it also at 88, but on a very different kind of green; and in spring of that same year Mr. W. J. Mure gained the silver cross at 86.

It is very pleasant to recall matches, or even special strokes or singular incidents, that will not occur twice in a lifetime, of which all golfers have so many. For example, the Lord Justice-Clerk (Lord Moncreiff) once told me that when he was playing a match with Lord Rutherfurd Clark, Mr. Donald Crawford, M.P., and Mr. Patrick Blair, W.S., his opponent's (Mr. Crawford) ball lay between 80 and 90 yards from the hole; the stick with the flag happened not to be quite in the hole, as it ought to have been, but about a foot from it. Crawford played with his cleek, struck the stick, and holed his ball. Lord Moncreiff played next, and performed exactly the same feat. He was a yard or two nearer. He also played with his cleek, struck the stick, and went in, thus halving the hole. According to the doctrine of chances, how unlikely this was! It may be mentioned, as a singular coincidence, that at the same hole, the week after, the Lord Justice-General, the chief of the other division of the Court of Session, holed his ball from about the same place off his short spoon, the Fates thus showing their impartiality by dealing their chances equally to both judges.

Again, I once, but only once, saw a long stroke played with the long spoon, and carry, not roll, into the hole, and remain there.

Another singular incident occurred when on one

occasion I was playing against Sir Hope Grant. We were going to the high hole coming home. Allan Robertson happened to be at the hole, and held up the stick. Sir Hope struck first, and went into the hole in one, on which Allan flung the flag into the air. I said, "Come, I have this for the half," and played. I went about a foot from the hole, and easily holed in two. I would have given a good deal to halve it in one; but there is no record of this ever having been done, and probably it never will be. We all know that the short hole has been occasionally done in one, but I have never heard of any other instance in which it was lost in two.[1]

I have played many exciting matches which I have forgotten all about, but one or two I have not forgotten. One I especially remember, having recorded it at the time. It was played on 24th and 25th August 1863, between George Condie and his

[1] While these sheets were in the press, this phenomenon has been repeated. On 4th February 1887, while Mr. Macfie and Mr. David Lamb were playing a match, going to the short hole out, Mr. Macfie laid his tee shot within six inches of the hole, but Mr. Lamb holed his in one—Mr. Macfie thus losing the hole in two.

brother-in-law, Major Boothby, against Mr. Hodge and myself. We were all then in the zenith of our game, and George Condie was as fine a gentleman player as was ever on the Links. We played for two days—three rounds the first day, and three rounds and a half the second, or 113 holes in all; and at the end of the 112th we were all even! Condie and Boothby gained the last hole.

A match that created a good deal of interest at the time arose from a challenge which appeared in the *Field* newspaper, from a father and son at Westward Ho, to play any other father and son in the country, the match to be three rounds of St. Andrews Links, on two consecutive days. My son Leslie and I accepted the challenge. The match was played on the 10th and 12th October 1874, in presence of a large gallery, and we had the satisfaction of beating them by seven holes.

A curious circumstance which happened to Major Chiene may be noticed. On one occasion when he was playing, his ball accidentally struck a swallow when on the wing, and killed it. The Major had the bird stuffed, and set upon the identical ball that killed it; it was placed as a curiosity in the Club-room, where it remained for many years.

Among the variety of incidents that have accompanied the play for the medal was one which occurred in 1860, when an extraordinary tempest raged. The wind from the north was howling, and the rain lashing. Just as parties were about to start a cry was heard that a vessel was being wrecked in the offing. The play for the medal was postponed. The lifeboat was launched; but there was great difficulty in getting it manned. Maitland Dougall, who was about to play, when he heard of the difficulty, volunteered to go, and took the stroke oar. The men were rescued, and the lifeboat came ashore in the afternoon. The play for the medal was begun after the arrival of the lifeboat. The wind was still furious. It was to Maitland Dougall's credit that, though his arms were sore, and he was stiff and all wet, he gained the Club gold medal at 112 strokes. Gourlay, the Musselburgh ball-maker, who was present, remarked, "What nerve the Captain must have for the game!" that he (Gourlay) would not have gone out in that boat for a thousand pounds.

A peculiar experience I myself once had in playing for the medal. I stood lowest for the Club gold medal, and Mr. Robert Clark, in playing the last hole home, lay near the road at one stroke fewer than I was. He played a pretty long stroke with his cleek, and actually *holed his ball*, thus tying with me for the medal! He gained the tie.

CHAPTER VII.

MERITS OF THE GAME.

DURING the course of these years the character of the game is a good deal altered. It happened that, coincident with the introduction of gutta-percha balls, a railway was opened through Fife, with a station at Leuchars, six miles from St. Andrews, from whence there was a service of omnibuses, and in a year or two afterwards a branch line was formed. This made St. Andrews, which had hitherto been rather a retired place of learned and ecclesiastical leisure, much more accessible. The consequence was that houses and villas quickly sprang up. Together, these influences had the effect of somewhat destroying the patrician and rather exclusive tone of the game. They so popularised it as to make it a game for all classes; and all classes do play at it—judges of the Supreme Court, officers of high rank in the Army and Navy, noblemen, tradesmen, men of all professions and of all ages, fathers and sons. I have seen a match played, the aggregate age of the players in which was

323. Nor is it in Scotland alone that the game is now played, but in many parts of England, where there are players that are quite first-class; in India and Canada also, and almost all the Colonies. A few years ago I followed a match that was being played on the famous heights of Abraham at Quebec.

Wherein do the charms of this game lie, that captivate youth, and retain their hold till far on in life? I have known the game survive all other sports—football and cricket, shooting, salmon-fishing, hunting, and deer-stalking. Probably it owes much to the variety of its attractions. It is a fine, open-air, athletic exercise, not violent, but bringing into play nearly all the muscles of the body; while that exercise can be continued for hours. But it would be a mistake to suppose that it is only muscular exertion that is required. It is a game of skill, needing mind and thought and judgment, as well as a cunning hand. It is also a social game, where one may go out with one friend or with three, as the case may be, and enjoy mutual intercourse, mingled with an excitement which is very pleasing, while it never requires to be associated with the degrading vice of gambling. It never palls or grows stale, as morning by morning the players appear at the teeing-ground with as keen a relish as if they had not seen a club for a month. Nor is it only while the game lasts that its zest is felt. How the player loves to recall the strokes and other incidents of the match, so that it is often played over again next morning while he is still in bed! But even more does it absorb the conversation of the evening. The late George Hughes wrote to his brother, the author of *Tom Brown's School-days*, trying to convert him to "Golfomania," as he called it; and speaking of the after-dinner conversation about the game, he says: "The humour of the whole thing was positively sublime. You have heard squires at their wine after a good run; bless you, they can't hold a candle to golfers. Most of the players were Scotch, and the earnestness with which the Scotch 'play' is a caution." This is true. How in the evening each dilates on his own wonderful strokes, and the singular chances that befell him in the different parts of the green!—all under the pleasurable delusion that every listener is as interested in his game as he himself is. How he tells of his long swipes, which he is not sure have ever been equalled, and of the perfect pitch which he made with the baffy, or iron, at the approach stroke, just carrying the bunker that intervened, and narrowly escaping the whins on the left! And then the long putt—how beautifully the ball rolled over the smooth green up to the very lip of the hole, or, more fortunate still, dropped into it! What putts! I remember Saddell once saying, as he looked at a fine putt that borrowed a little from the side of the undulating ground, and dribbled gently down, down, down into the hole, "What a splendid putt! In my time I have had the best grouse-shooting in Scotland, and the best salmon river, and the best deer-stalking, and I have kept the best hunters at Melton; but I am thankful to say I can now dream about a putt!"

But I must close these reminiscences. To recall such memories has been both pleasant and pathetic —pleasant because they have brought back the sunny hours of recreation in a busy and a happy life; pathetic, because they have been associated with so many who are now gone. How quickly these forty-five years have receded into the past! and now, looking back on them, one naturally sympathises with the Roman poet when he says:

> Eheu! fugaces, Posthume, Posthume,
> Labuntur anni.

APPENDIX.

Royal and Ancient Golf Club, St. Andrews

INSTITUTED 14TH MAY 1754.

LIST OF CAPTAINS AND MEDAL-HOLDERS.

CAPTAINS.

WINNERS OF THE SILVER CLUB.

Year.	Names.
1754.	William Landale, Esq., Merchant, St. Andrews.
1755.	Thomas Boswall, Esq., Writer in Edinburgh.
1756.	Alexander Duncan, Esq. of Craigton, Edinburgh.
1757.	
1758.	Hugh Fraser, Esq. of Lovat.
1759.	Sir James Carnegie, Bart., M.P.
1760.	
1761.	Alexander Duncan, Esq. of Craigton, Advocate.
1762.	Hugh Fraser, Esq. of Lovat.
1763.	Sir Harry Seton, Bart.
1764.	William St. Clair, Esq. of Roslin.
1765.	The Hon. Francis Charteris of Amisfield.
1766.	William St. Clair, Esq. of Roslin.
1767.	James Durham, Esq. of Largo.
1768.	William St. Clair, Esq. of Roslin.
1769.	Dr. George Forrest, Professor of Civil History in the United College, St. Andrews.
1770.	Henry Bethune, Esq. of Nydie.
1771.	Ninian Imrie, Esq. of Denmuir.
1772.	James Morrison, Esq. of Naughton.

Year.	Names.
1773.	Patrick Rigg, Esq. of Downfield.
1774.	John Hay, Esq. of Leys.
1775.	The Right Hon. the Earl of Balcarres.
1776.	Roger Aytoun, Esq. of Inchdairnie.
1777.	John Balfour, Esq. of Fernie.
1778.	Walter Boswell, Esq.
1779.	James Morrison, Esq. of Naughton.
1780.	James Durham, Esq. of Largo.
1781.	Alexander Duncan, Esq.
1782.	The Earl of Balcarres.
1783.	Major William Morrison.
1784.	Robert Low, Esq. of Clatto.
1785.	Captain John Cheape of Rossie.
1786.	Colonel John Thomson of Charlton.
1787.	James Cheape, Esq. of Strathtyrum.
1788.	Captain James Dalrymple.
1789.	Captain William Nairne.
1790.	Patrick Rigg, Esq. of Downfield.
1791.	Alexander Duncan, Esq.
1792.	The Right Hon. the Earl of Crawford.
1793.	John Pattullo, Esq. of Balhouffie.
1794.	Captain Alexander Aytone of Kippo.
1795.	Alexander Anderson, Esq. of Newbigging.
1796.	James Morrison, Esq. of Naughton.
1797.	Thomas Erskine, Esq. of Cambo.
1798.	Methven Erskine, Esq. of Airdrie.
1799.	John Dalyell, Esq.
1800.	Robert Pattullo, Esq.
1801.	George Cheape, Esq.
1802.	Hugh Cleghorn, Esq. of Stravithy.
1803.	George Paterson, Esq. of Cunnoquhie.
1804.	John Anstruther Thomson, Esq. of Charlton.
1805.	Colonel David Dewar of Gilston.
1806.	William Dalgleish, Esq. of Scotscraig.
1807.	General George Moncrieff.
1808.	Alexander Guthrie, Esq. of Craigie.
1809.	James Home Rigg, Esq. of Morton.
1810.	John Maitland, Esq. of Kilmaron.

Year.	Names.
1811.	Thomas Bruce, Esq. of Grangemuir.
1812.	R. Gillespie Smyth, Esq. of Gibleston.
1813.	General James Durham of Largo.
1814.	George Cheape, Esq. of Pusk.
1815.	John Makgill, Esq. of Kemback.
1816.	Sir John Anstruther of Anstruther, Bart.
1817.	David Moncrieffe, Esq., younger of Moncrieffe.
1818.	John Murray, Esq. of Lintrose.
1819.	Robert Bruce, Esq. of Kennet.
1820.	The Right Hon. David, Earl of Leven and Melville.
1821.	Colonel Alexander Bethune of Blebo.
1822.	Alexander Binny, Esq. St. Andrews.
1823.	John Whyte-Melville, Esq. of Strathkinness.
1824.	Colonel James Lindsay of Balcarres.
1825.	Sir Ralph Anstruther of Balcaskie, Bart.
1826.	Charles M. Christie, Esq. of Durie.
1827.	James Cheape, Esq. of Balgove, Captain R.N
1828.	John Dalyell, Esq. of Lingo.
1829.	Sir David Erskine of Cambo, Bart.
1830.	Francis Balfour, Esq. of Fernie.
1831.	James Stuart Oliphant, Esq. of Rossie.
1832.	C. Halket Craigie, Esq. of Dumbarnie.
1833.	Major Robert Anstruther of Third Part.
1834.	General Sir John Oswald of Dunnikier, G.C.B.
1835.	Colonel J. Murray Belshes of Buttergask.
1836.	Do. do.
1837.	George Moncrieff, Esq., Captain Scots Fusilier Guards.
1838.	O. T. Bruce, Esq. of Falkland.
1839.	John Grant, Esq. of Kilgraston.
1840.	Henry Stewart, Esq. of St. Fort.
1841.	David Gillespie, Esq. of Mountquhannie.
1842.	John Balfour, Esq. of Balbirnie.
1843.	Sir David Baird of Newbyth, Bart.
1844.	Sir Thomas Moncrieffe of Moncrieffe, Bart.
1845.	George Makgill, Esq. of Kemback.
1846.	Robert Lindsay, Esq. of Straiton.
1847.	F. L. S. Wedderburn, Esq. of Wedderburn.
1848.	James Wolfe Murray, Esq. of Cringletie.

Year.	Names.
1849.	James Townsend Oswald, Esq. of Dunnikier.
1850.	James O. Fairlie, Esq. of Coodham.
1851.	George Whyte-Melville, Esq. yr. of Mount Melville.
1852.	E. J. Jackson, Esq.
1853.	The Right Hon. the Earl of Eglinton and Winton, K.T.
1854.	Hay Erskine Wemyss, Esq. of Wemyss and Torrie.
1855.	Lord Loughborough.
1856.	Sir Hugh Lyon Playfair.
1857.	Robert Cathcart, Esq., younger of Pitcairly.
1858.	John Anstruther Thomson, Esq. of Charlton.
1859.	Sir David Baird of Newbyth, Bart.
1860.	Sir Thomas Erskine of Cambo, Bart.
1861.	George Dempster, Esq. of Skibo.
1862.	The Right Hon. the Earl of Dalhousie, K.T.
1863.	His Royal Highness the Prince of Wales.
1864.	Viscount Dupplin.
1865.	Lieutenant-General Sir John Low of Clatto.
1866.	Sir Robert Anstruther of Balcaskie, Bart.
1867.	Sir John T. Bethune of Kilconquhar, Bart.
1868.	Sir Coutts Lindsay of Balcarres, Bart.
1869.	Alexander Bethune, Esq. of Blebo.
1870.	Sir Robert Hay, Bart., of Hayston and Kingsmeadows.
1871.	John Blackwood, Esq.
1872.	Alexander Kinloch, Esq., younger of Gilmerton.
1873.	William Baillie Skene, Esq. of Pitlour.
1874.	The Right Hon. William Patrick Adam of Blair-Adam, M.P.
1875.	The Hon. Charles Carnegie.
1876.	His Royal Highness Prince Leopold.
1877.	The Right Hon. John Inglis of Glencorse.
1878.	The Hon. George Waldegrave Leslie.
1879.	The Right Hon. the Earl of Elgin and Kincardine.
1880.	The Right Hon. the Earl of Glasgow.
1881.	Captain Randall Jackson.
1882.	The Hon. Robert Preston Bruce.
1883.	Vacant.
1884.	George Glennie, Esq.
1885.	The Earl of Aberdeen.
1886.	Captain Daniel Shaw Stewart.

WINNERS OF THE GOLD MEDAL

PRESENTED BY HIS LATE MAJESTY KING WILLIAM IV.

First Competed for in 1837.

Year.	Names.	Strokes.
1837.	J. Stuart Oliphant, Esq.,	104
1838.	Captain J. Hope Grant,	100
1839.	J. H. Wood, Esq., Leith,	99
1840.	Major H. L. Playfair,	105
1841.	Sir David Baird, Bart.,	100
1842.	James Condie, Esq.,	103
1843.	W. M. Goddard, Esq., Leith,	103
1844.	J. Hamilton Dundas, Esq.,	111
1845.	James Calvert, Esq.,	100
1846.	Do. do.,	111
1847.	N. J. Ferguson Blair, Esq.,	105
1848.	George Condie, Esq., Perth,	104
1849.	W. M. Goddard, Esq.,	105
1850.	Sir David Baird, Bart.,	100
1851.	O'Brian B. Peter, Esq., Kirkland,	105
1852.	Robert Hay, Esq.,	99
1853.	John C. Stewart, Esq., 72d Highlanders,	90
1854.	William Archibald Hamilton, Esq.,	97
1855.	George Glennie, Esq.,	88
1856.	Captain W. H. Maitland Dougall,	92
1857.	James Ogilvie Fairlie, Esq. of Coodham,	101
1858.	Patrick Alexander, Esq.,	96
1859.	Thomas D. M'Whannell, Esq.,	96
1860.	William C. Thomson, Esq., Dundee,	104
1861.	Thomas D. M'Whannell, Esq.,	98
1862.	James Ogilvie Fairlie, Esq. of Coodham,	99
1863.	Captain W. H. Maitland Dougall,	95
1864.	Robert Clark, Esq., Edinburgh,	94
1865.	Captain W. H. Maitland Dougall,	92
1866.	Thomas Hodge, Esq.,	97
1867.	Do. do.,	96

Year.	Names.	Strokes.
1868.	Charles Anderson, Esq., ...	95
1869.	Thomas Hodge, Esq., ...	89
1870.	Gilbert Mitchell Innes, Esq., ...	89
1871.	Thomas Mackay, Esq., ...	91
1872.	Sir Robert Hay, Bart., ...	94
1873.	Henry A. Lamb, Esq., ...	92
1874.	Samuel Mure Fergusson, Esq., ...	91
1875.	Leslie M. Balfour, Esq., ...	93
1876.	Do. do., ...	91
1877.	Do. do., ...	89
1878.	Henry A. Lamb, Esq., ...	90
1879.	Charles Anderson, Esq., ...	88
1880.	Alexander Stuart, Esq., ...	89
1881.	Samuel Mure Fergusson, Esq., ...	90
1882.	Alexander Stuart, Esq., ...	88
1883.	Leslie M. Balfour, Esq., ...	88
1884.	Horace Hutchinson, Esq., ...	87
1885.	John Ernest Laidlay, Esq., ...	87
1886.	Samuel Mure Fergusson, Esq., ...	84

WINNERS OF THE GOLD MEDALS

Given by the Club.

I.—From 1806 to 1836.

During which period this Medal was the only one competed for.

1806.	Walter Cook, Esq., W.S., ...	100
1807.	Do. do., ...	101
1808.	William Oliphant, Esq., ...	102
1809.	Do. do., ...	103
1810.	Dr. James Hunter, United College, St. Andrews,	111
1811.	Do. do. do.,	116
1812.	Robert Pattullo, Esq., of Balhouffie, . .	109
1813.	Do. do., . .	114
1814.	Do. do., . .	118

Year.	Names.	Strokes.
1815.	Dr. James Hunter, United College, St. Andrews,	101
1816.	David Moncrieffe, Esq., yr. of Moncrieffe,	111
1817.	Walter Cook, Esq., W.S.,	113
1818.	Captain H. L. Playfair,	111
1819.	Sir David Moncrieffe, Bart., of Moncrieffe,	102
1820.	Edward D'Oyley, Esq.,	108
1821.	Henry M. Low, Esq., W.S.,	108
1822.	Charles Shaw, Esq., Leith,	109
1823.	Henry M. Low, Esq., W.S.,	120
1824.	Do. do.,	110
1825.	Samuel Messieux, Esq.,	105
1826.	Robert Pattullo, Esq., Jun.,	104
1827.	Samuel Messieux, Esq.,	111
1828.	Robert Pattullo, Esq., Jun.,	105
1829.	Major Holcroft, R.A.,	109
1830.	Do. do.,	111
1831.	David Duncan, Esq., Rosemount,	111
1832.	John H. Wood, Esq., Leith,	104
1833.	Major Holcroft, R.A.,	103
1834.	Robert Oliphant, Esq., younger of Rossie,	97
1835.	Do. do.,	105
1836.	Major William Wemyss,	104

II.—From 1837.

When the Medal became the Second Prize at the Autumn General Meeting.

1837.	James Condie, Esq., Perth,	103
1838.	Robert Haig, Esq.,	112
1839.	Andrew Stirling, Esq.,	99
1840.	William Wood, Esq.,	105
1841.	Captain Archibald Ogilvy Dalgliesh,	109
1842.	Major H. L. Playfair,	108
1843.	William Buist, Esq.,	103
1844.	James Skelton, Esq.,	112
1845.	N. J. Ferguson Blair, Esq.,	102
1846.	William Buist, Esq.,	112

Year.	Names.	Strokes.
1847.	James Calvert, Esq., ...	106
1848.	Captain David Campbell, ...	105
1849.	Sir David Baird, Bart., of Newbyth, . .	107
1850.	George Condie, Esq., ...	100
1851.	Robert Hay, Esq., ...	110
1852.	Thomas Peter, Esq., Kirkland, . . .	101
1853.	James Balfour, Esq., Edinburgh, . . .	93
1854.	Patrick Alexander, Esq., ...	100
1855.	William C. Thomson, Esq., ...	93
1856.	Captain Robert T. Boothby, Perth, . .	94
1857.	James Balfour, Esq., Edinburgh, . . .	101
1858.	Robert Mitchell, Esq., St. Andrews, . .	98
1859.	Captain W. H. Maitland Dougall, . .	97
1860.	Do. do., ...	112
1861.	James Balfour, Esq., Edinburgh, . . .	102
1862.	Thomas D. M'Whannell, Esq., . . .	101
1863.	Robert Clark, Esq., Edinburgh, . . .	98
1864.	Captain W. H. Maitland Dougall, . .	99
1865.	Dr. Argyll Robertson, ...	97
1866.	David J. Lamb, Esq., ...	97
1867.	Dr. Duncan M'Cuaig, ...	96
1868.	Captain J. C. Stewart of Fasnacloich, . .	97
1869.	Dr. Duncan M'Cuaig, ...	94
1870.	Dr. Douglas Argyll Robertson, . . .	89
1871.	Do. do., ...	97
1872.	Do. do., ...	97
1873.	Do. do., ...	93
1874.	Leslie Melville Balfour, Esq., . . .	97
1875.	Major Robert T. Boothby, ...	93
1876.	Alexander Stuart, Esq., ...	92
1877.	Samuel Mure Fergusson, Esq., . . .	94
1878.	Charles Anderson, Esq., ...	90
1879.	David I. Lamb, Esq., ...	89
1880.	Leslie M. Balfour, Esq., ...	91
1881.	Do. do., ...	91
1882.	Thomas Mackay, Esq., ...	88
1883.	Charles E. S. Chambers, Esq., . . .	94
1884.	Henry Johnston, Esq., ...	91
1885.	Leslie Melville Balfour, Esq., . . .	88
1886.	John Ernest Laidlay, Esq., ...	87

WINNERS OF THE SILVER CROSS

PRESENTED BY COLONEL J. MURRAY BELSHES OF BUTTERGASK.

First competed for in 1836.

Year.	Names.	Strokes.
1836.	James Condie, Esq., Perth,	110
1837.	John H. Wood, Esq., Leith,	100
1838.	C. Robertson, Esq.,	108
1839.	Do. do.,	104
1840.	Samuel Messieux, Esq.,	109
1841.	Robert Haig, Esq.,	104
1842.	Do. do.,	104
1843.	Captain David Campbell,	103
1844.	Robert Haig, Esq.,	111
1845.	Captain A. O. Dalgliesh,	99
1846.	Robert Lindsay, Esq.,	110
1847.	Captain David Campbell,	104
1848.	Robert Hay, Esq.,	101
1849.	J. O. Fairlie, Esq.,	100
1850.	George Condie, Esq., Perth,	96
1851.	George Glennie, Esq.,	99
1852.	Captain W. H. Maitland Dougall, Scotscraig,	96
1853.	Henry Jelf Sharpe, Esq.,	96
1854.	J. O. Fairlie, Esq.,	95
1855.	Captain W. H. Maitland Dougall,	98
1856.	William Playfair, Esq.,	102
1857.	W. C. Thomson, Esq.,	96
1858.	Sir Thomas Moncrieffe of Moncrieffe, Bart.,	95
1859.	James C. Lindsay, Esq., Broughty-Ferry,	101
1860.	James Ogilvie Fairlie, Esq. of Coodham,	99
1861.	Thomas Hodge, Esq.,	92
1862.	Henry Mackechnie, Esq.,	94
1863.	Gilbert Mitchell Innes, Esq.,	97
1864.	William C. Thomson, Esq.,	95
1865.	Gilbert Mitchell Innes, Esq.,	98

E

Year.	Names.	Strokes.
1866.	William C. Thomson, Esq., ...	92
1867.	Robert Clark, Esq., ...	92
1868.	Major Robert T. Boothby, ...	92
1869.	Robert Clark, Esq., ...	92
1870.	Do. do., ...	92
1871.	Henry Lamb, Esq., ...	93
1872.	Ross W. Ochterlony, Esq., ...	98
1873.	Henry A. Lamb, Esq., ...	99
1874.	William J. Mure, Esq., ...	90
1875.	Captain Alexander Dingwall Fordyce, . .	92
1876.	Major Robert T. Boothby, ...	92
1877.	William J. Mure, Esq., ...	97
1878.	A. Frank Simson, Esq., ...	89
1879.	William J. Mure, Esq., ...	86
1880.	Charles Anderson, Esq., ...	87
1881.	Elliot S. Balfour, Esq., ...	88
1882.	Alexander Stuart, Esq., ...	88
1883.	Do. do., ...	83
1884.	William S. Wilson, Esq., ...	91
1885.	S. Mure Fergusson, Esq., ...	89
1886.	Bruce E. Goff, Esq., ...	90

GEORGE GLENNIE MEDAL.

1881. S. Mure Fergusson, Esq., ...

Note.—The Medal was won this year by the winner of the Royal Medal—the present mode of winning it not having been decided on.

1882.	Alexander Stuart, Esq., ...	176
1883.	Leslie Melville Balfour, Esq., ...	173
1884.	Horace G. Hutchinson, Esq., ...	178
1885.	Leslie Melville Balfour, Esq., ...	178
1886.	Do. do., ...	181

WINNERS OF THE SILVER MEDAL

PRESENTED BY THE GOLFING SOCIETY OF BOMBAY.

First competed for in 1846.

Year.	Names.	Strokes
1846.	William Buist, Esq., ...	111
1847.	George Dempster, Esq., ...	111
1848.	J. O. Fairlie, Esq., ...	104
1849.	John Campbell, Esq. of Glensaddel, . . .	101
1850.	Captain Heriot Maitland (afterwards Maitland Dougall), Ramornie, ...	101
1851.	Do. do., . .	103
1852.	John Campbell, Esq., of Glensaddel, . .	98
1853.	J. O. Fairlie, Esq., ...	96
1854.	Captain W. H. Maitland Dougall, . .	98
1855.	James Condie, Esq., ...	98
1856.	Captain W. H. Maitland Dougall, . .	105
1857.	Do. do., . . .	94
1858.	Alexander Bethune, Esq. of Blebo, . .	99
1859.	William C. Thomson, Esq., Dundee, . .	102
1860.	Captain W. H. Maitland Dougall, . .	98
1861.	Major R. T. Boothby, ...	101
1862.	Thomas Hodge, Esq., ...	97
1863.	Robert Clark, Esq., Edinburgh, . . .	100
1864.	Gilbert Mitchell Innes, Esq., . . .	101
1865.	Robert Clark, Esq., ...	94
1866.	Thomas D. M'Whannell, Esq., . . .	95
1867.	Dr. D. Argyll Robertson, ...	94
1868.	Charles Anderson, Esq., ...	95
1869.	Captain W. H. Maitland Dougall, . .	93
1870.	David J. Lamb, Esq., ...	95
1871.	Dr. Douglas Argyll Robertson, . . .	93
1872.	William C. Thomson, Esq., ...	98
1873.	Thomas Hodge, Esq., ...	99
1874.	Gilbert Mitchell Innes, Esq., . . .	90
1875.	William J. Mure, Esq., ...	97

Year.	Names.	Strokes.
1876.	Leslie M. Balfour, Esq., ...	98
1877.	George M. Cox, Esq., ...	97
1878.	Charles Anderson, Esq., ...	93
1879.	Leslie M. Balfour, Esq., ...	94
1880.	Do. do., ...	87
1881.	James Hay Blackwell, Jun., Esq., . .	89
1882.	David I. Lamb, Esq., ...	88
1883.	Leslie M. Balfour, Esq., ...	85
1884.	Horace Hutchinson, Esq., ...	91
1885.	Leslie M. Balfour, Esq., ...	90
1886.	Rev. R. A. Hull, ...	91

CALCUTTA CUP (HANDICAP TOURNAMENT).

1885. Major W. B. Craigie, ...
1886. A. F. Macfie, Esq., ...

Afterword
by
Jack Nicklaus

I haven't read a lot of golf history, but the thing that has struck me most from what I have learned about the game's past is how unchanging its appeal has remained through its many centuries of physical refinement and reshaping.

James Balfour's lovely little book about St. Andrews golf in his time seems to me a classic example of this. The course, the customs, the competitions, the costumes, the implements, and almost everything else he writes about will seem very foreign and antique to those who know only the modern American game—as, despite its elegance, might also his literary style. But leaping from every page comes exactly the same commitment to and joy in whatever it is that constitutes the magic of golf that you and I feel today. Therein lies a bond that time and change seem never able to impair. James Balfour was an absolute golf nut, and that makes him one with us.

I am no authority on such things, but would guess that this book offers as good an overview of golf's most dramatic evolutionary period as it is possible to come by. But for me as a player and designer of golf courses, its most enjoyable passages are those describing what happened in that time to what we now know as the Old Course.

Like most golfers, I was aware that things had changed since someone first swung a long stick at a small ball in the Kingdom of Fife, but I had no idea of specifically what or how much. Having those blanks filled was enjoyable, and will be even more so the next time I tee it up in my favorite place in the whole world to play golf. As now enlightened I shall look upon the holes with new perspective, and try to imagine their texture and challenge when Mr. Balfour liked them better. And, if that be possible, I will probably love St. Andrews even more.

Jack Nicklaus